Where in the World Can I . . .

DIG UP A FOSSIL?

Where in the World Can I . . .

DIG UP A FOSSIL?

www.worldbook.com

World Book, Inc.
180 North LaSalle Street, Suite 900
Chicago, Illinois 60601
USA

For information about other World Book publications, visit our website at **www.worldbook.com** or call **1-800-WORLDBK (967-5325).**

For information about sales to schools and libraries, call 1-800-975-3250 (United States), or 1-800-837-5365 (Canada).

Library of Congress Cataloging-in-Publication Data for this volume has been applied for.

Where in the World Can I...
ISBN: 978-0-7166-2178-2 (set, hc.)

Dig Up a Fossil?
ISBN: 978-0-7166-2181-2 (hc.)

Also available as:
ISBN: 978-0-7166-2191-1 (e-book)

1st printing July 2018

STAFF

Writer: Shawn Brennan

Executive Committee

President
Jim O'Rourke

Vice President and Editor in Chief
Paul A. Kobasa

Vice President, Finance
Donald D. Keller

Vice President, Marketing
Jean Lin

Vice President, International Sales
Maksim Rutenberg

Vice President, Technology
Jason Dole

Director, Human Resources
Bev Ecker

Editorial

Director, New Print
Tom Evans

Managing Editor, New Print
Jeff De La Rosa

Senior Editor, New Print
Shawn Brennan

Editor, New Print
Grace Guibert

Librarian
S. Thomas Richardson

Manager, Contracts & Compliance (Rights & Permissions)
Loranne K. Shields

Manager, Indexing Services
David Pofelski

Digital

Director, Digital Produ
Development
Erika Meller

Manager, Digital Prod
Jonathan Wills

Graphics and Design

Senior Art Director
Tom Evans

Coordinator, Design Development and Production
Brenda Tropinski

Media Researcher
Rosalia Bledsoe

Manufacturing/ Production

Manufacturing Manage
Anne Fritzinger

Proofreader
Nathalie Strassheim

TABLE OF CONTENTS

WHAT IS A FOSSIL?

A fossil is the remains of a living thing that died a very time long ago. A fossil can be thousands or millions of years old. Fossils help scientists learn about plants and animals that lived in the past.

Most of those living things became *extinct*—that is, they died off completely—long ago. Fossils are one of the main ways that scientists learn about *prehistoric* life. Prehistoric means the time before people began to write about the things living and happening around them.

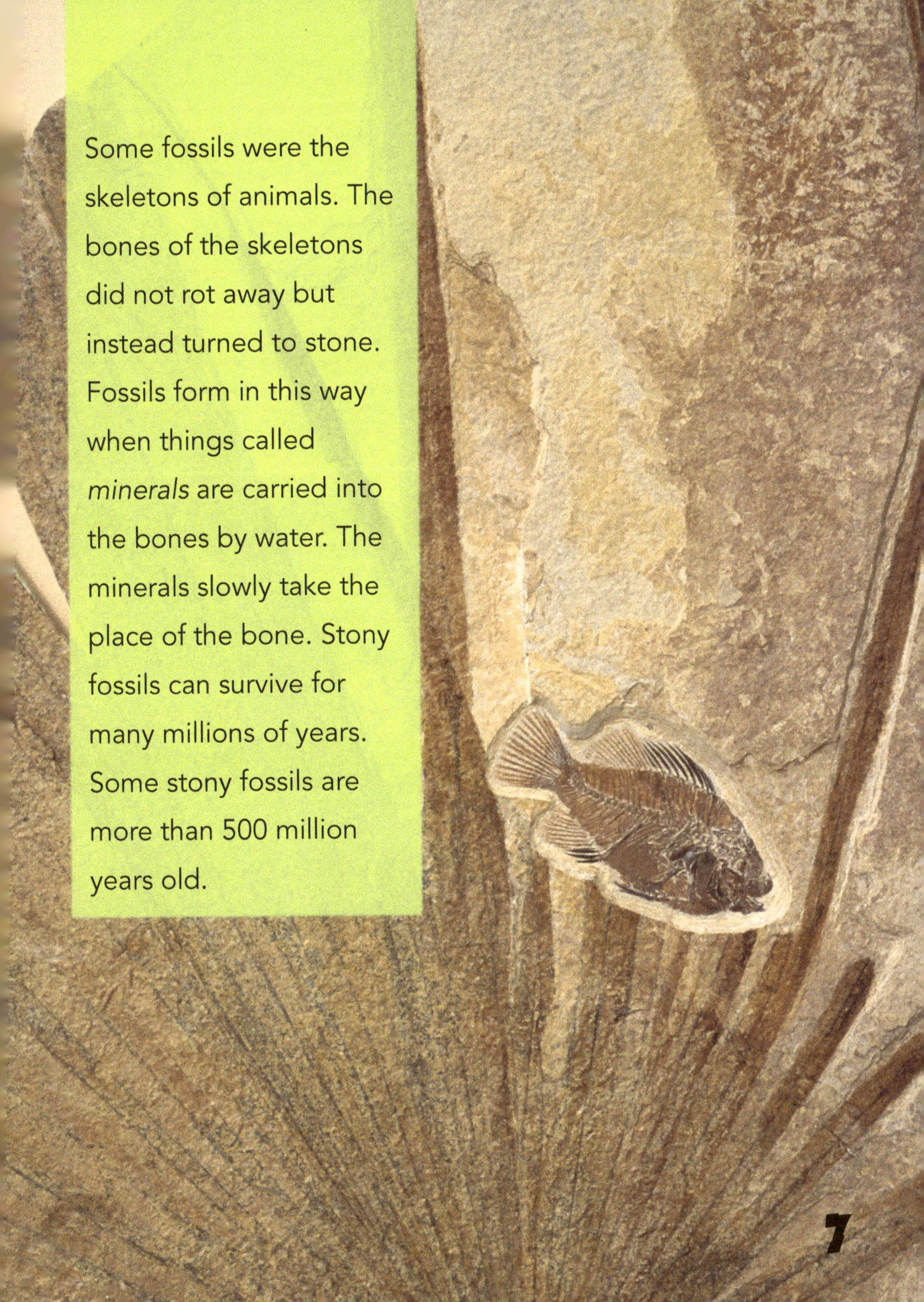

Some fossils were the skeletons of animals. The bones of the skeletons did not rot away but instead turned to stone. Fossils form in this way when things called *minerals* are carried into the bones by water. The minerals slowly take the place of the bone. Stony fossils can survive for many millions of years. Some stony fossils are more than 500 million years old.

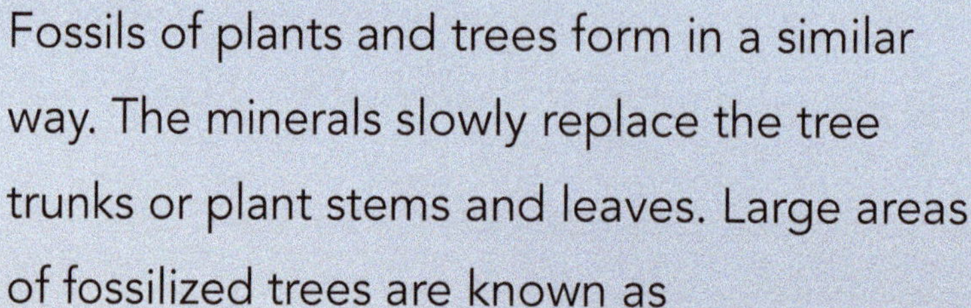

Fossils of plants and trees form in a similar way. The minerals slowly replace the tree trunks or plant stems and leaves. Large areas of fossilized trees are known as *petrified forests.* Some petrified forests are more than 200 million years old.

The stone shows many details of the original wood.

Other fossils are marks called *impressions.* These fossils show only the outline of a living thing. Impressions form after a living thing dies in mud and is covered with layer after layer of mud and soil. Over millions of years, the mud gets pressed down and turns into rock. A flattened print of the living thing stays in the rock. Most fossils of plants and of animals without bones formed in this way.

Fossils of plants and animals called *molds* also form after the plant or animal is buried in mud. Instead of being pushed flat, though, the plants and animals kept their shape as the mud around them turned to stone. Over time, water washed away the animal or plant parts. This leaves a space with the living thing's shape in the stone. Sometimes, minerals have filled the space. That creates a fossil called a *cast*. A cast is like a sculpture made of stone.

There also are other kinds of fossils. A hardened sap called *amber* can preserve pollen and other plant parts. Plants and animals may be preserved in tar pits. Fossils may also be preserved in permanently frozen ground. Scientists have even found bits of plants in the guts of frozen *mammoths* (giant prehistoric elephants) that became extinct thousands of years ago.

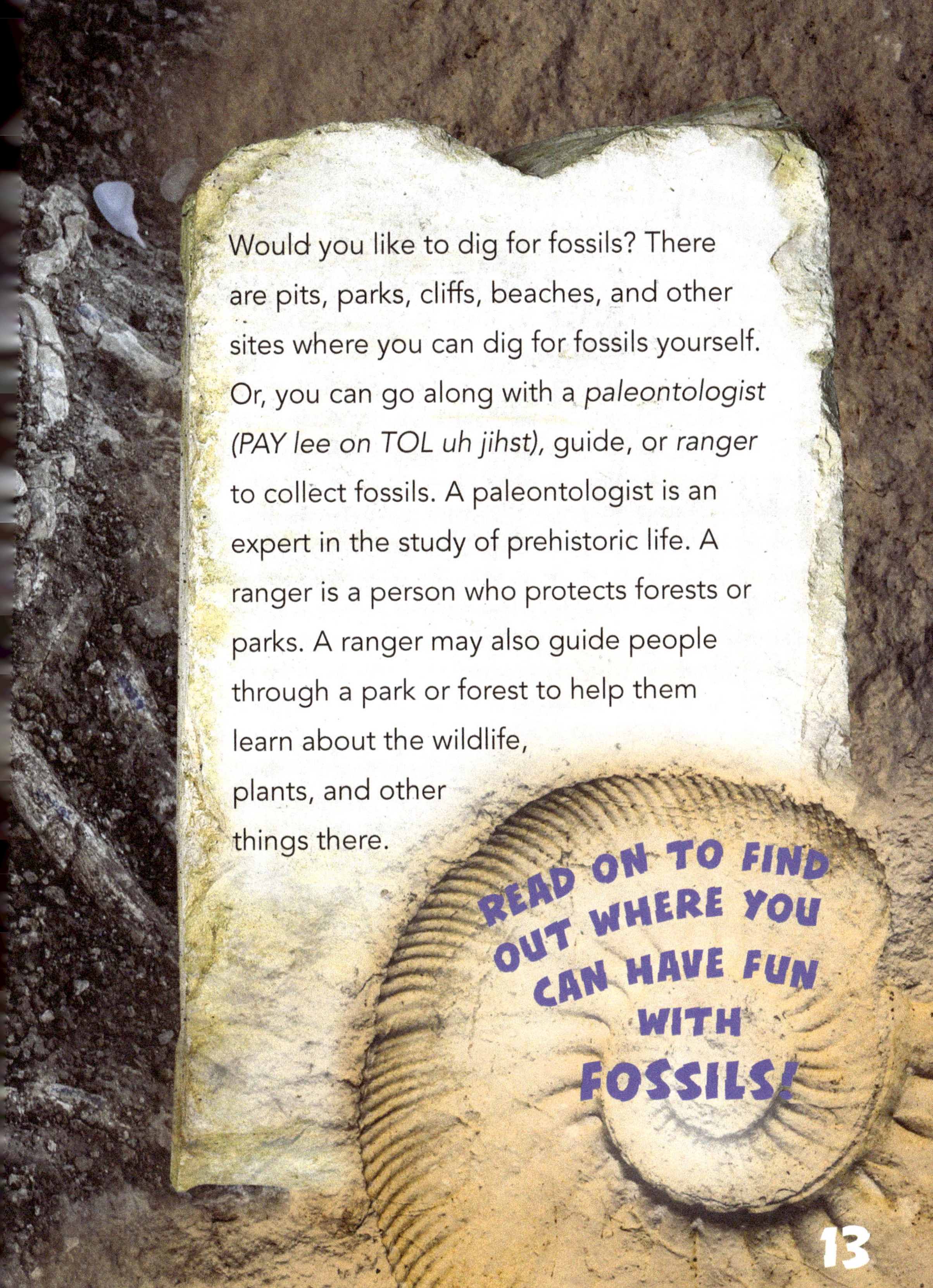

Would you like to dig for fossils? There are pits, parks, cliffs, beaches, and other sites where you can dig for fossils yourself. Or, you can go along with a *paleontologist (PAY lee on TOL uh jihst)*, guide, or *ranger* to collect fossils. A paleontologist is an expert in the study of prehistoric life. A ranger is a person who protects forests or parks. A ranger may also guide people through a park or forest to help them learn about the wildlife, plants, and other things there.

READ ON TO FIND OUT WHERE YOU CAN HAVE FUN WITH FOSSILS!

MONTOUR PRESERVE FOSSIL PIT

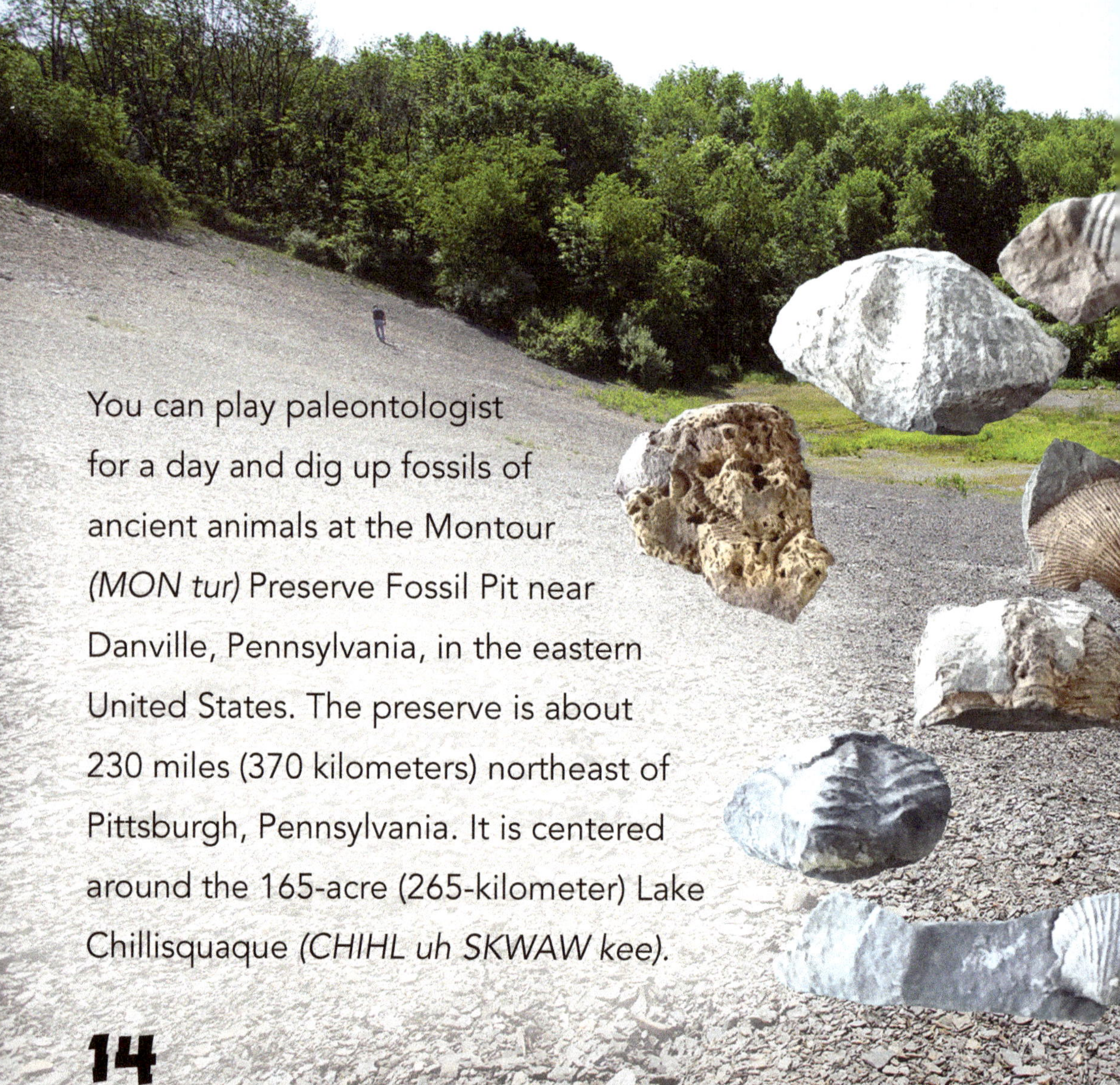

You can play paleontologist for a day and dig up fossils of ancient animals at the Montour *(MON tur)* Preserve Fossil Pit near Danville, Pennsylvania, in the eastern United States. The preserve is about 230 miles (370 kilometers) northeast of Pittsburgh, Pennsylvania. It is centered around the 165-acre (265-kilometer) Lake Chillisquaque *(CHIHL uh SKWAW kee).*

The Montour Preserve was founded in 1972. It is managed by the Montour Area Recreation Commission. The preserve includes a nature center and miles or kilometers of hiking trails. The fossil pit is open to the public the year around, admission is free, and you may keep any fossils you find!

The Montour Fossil Pit is made up of about one acre (0.4 hectare) of *shale.* Shale is a type of rock that is buried underground. It is made up of fine *grains* (very tiny bits). Shales can be broken easily into thin layers. Shale is mostly a hard mineral called *quartz* and minerals that are found in clay. It is formed when mud is pressed into thin, hard layers. Long ago, plants and animals were often buried in this mud and formed impressions, molds, and casts. We can find some of these plants and animals preserved in shale today.

There are a lot of sea animal fossils in the shale in the Montour Preserve Fossil Pit. These shales were formed about 395 million years ago when much of what today is the state of Pennsylvania was covered by a warm, shallow sea. This time in Earth's history is called the Devonian *(duh VOH nee uhn)* Period. It lasted from about 416 million to 359 million years ago. This period was many millions of years before the first dinosaurs lived.

Living things had only begun to appear on land at this time. The first trees developed during this period. The first insects and four-legged animals also appeared. These animals and plants probably could not live far from the water. In the oceans, the first sharks appeared. Most of the land formed just two large continents in the Devonian Period. They were separated by a narrow sea.

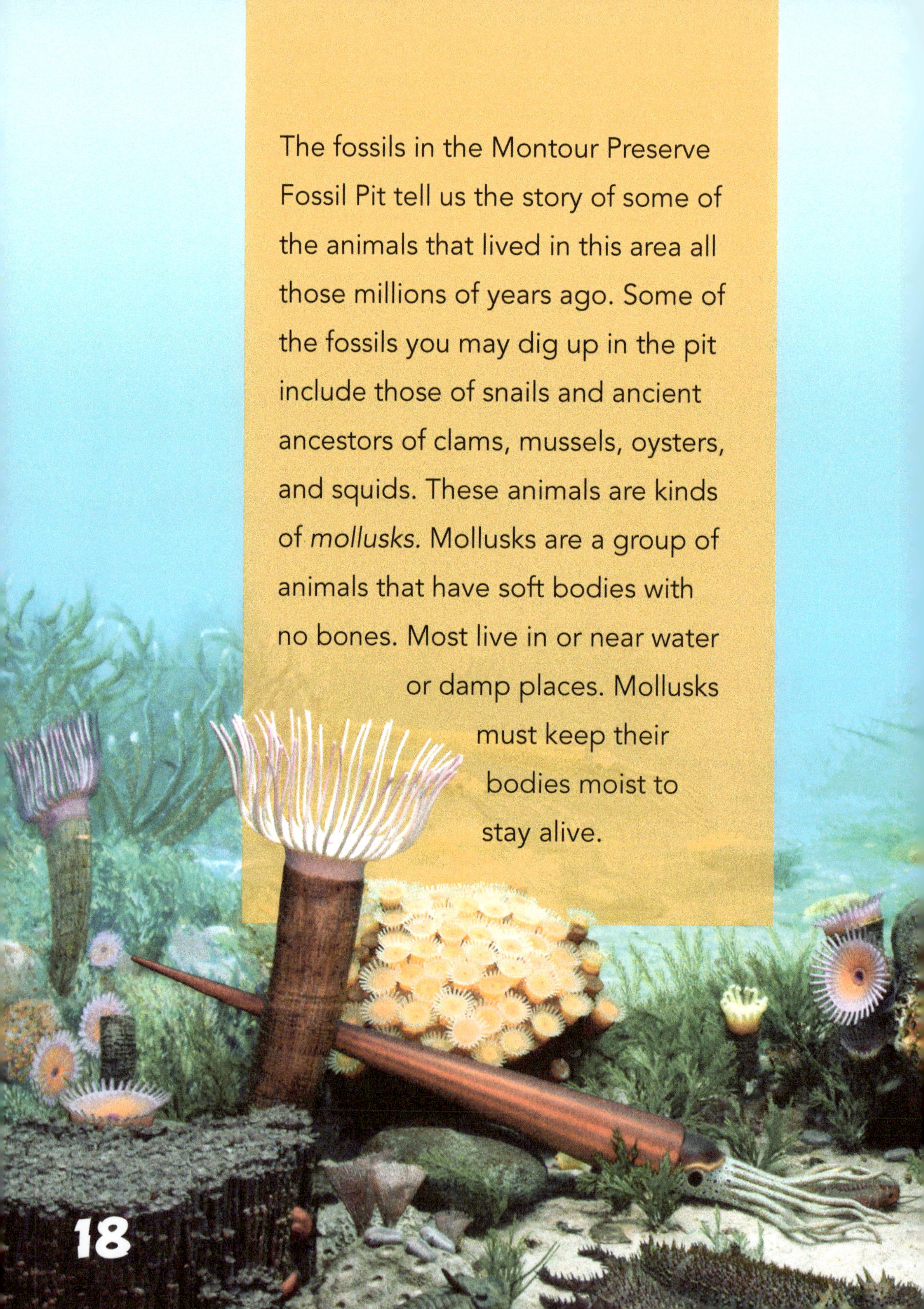

The fossils in the Montour Preserve Fossil Pit tell us the story of some of the animals that lived in this area all those millions of years ago. Some of the fossils you may dig up in the pit include those of snails and ancient ancestors of clams, mussels, oysters, and squids. These animals are kinds of *mollusks.* Mollusks are a group of animals that have soft bodies with no bones. Most live in or near water or damp places. Mollusks must keep their bodies moist to stay alive.

You may also find fossils of sea animals called *corals (KAWR uhlz)* and *crinoids (KRY noydz).* Corals live together in groups called *colonies.* They are related to jellyfish and sea *anemones (uh NEHM uh neez).* Sea anemones are ocean animals that look like flowers. Crinoids also look like flowers. They are sometimes called sea lilies. They have featherlike arms. Crinoids are related to spiny animals like starfish and sea urchins.

The Montour Preserve Fossil Pit is especially famous for its fossils of prehistoric sea animals called *trilobites (TRY luh byts).* There are so many of these fossils around here that the trilobite is the state fossil of Pennsylvania! But trilobites lived in all parts of the world. They lived from about 542 million years ago to about 251 million years ago.

Trilobites are related to the horseshoe crabs that are alive today. A soft shell covered much of the trilobite's body. Two grooves divided the shell lengthwise into three sections. The body had three main parts: the head, the *thorax* (middle section), and the tail. The thorax had many *segments,* or parts. Each segment had legs. Trilobites breathed through gills on their legs. Most trilobites were under 4 inches (10 centimeters) long. However, some were much larger.

Trilobites died out at the end of the *Permian (PUR mee uhn)* Period. This time lasted from around 299 million to 251 million years ago. During this time, one of the worst extinctions in Earth's history happened. Most animals and plants died out. But they left behind many fossils for us to find and study. The plants and animals that survived spread and developed into many new kinds of living things. Read on to learn about what fossils tell us about other times in Earth's history!

OTHER PLACES TO DIG UP FOSSILS

JOGGINS FOSSIL CLIFFS

You can find fossils from the time just after the Devonian Period at Joggins Fossil Cliffs in the province of Nova Scotia *(NOH vuh SKOH shuh)* in eastern Canada. This time is called the *Carboniferous (kahr buh NIHF uhr uhs)* Period. It lasted from about 359 million to 299 million years ago. This was still many millions of years before the first dinosaurs were stomping around. Joggins has some of the highest tides in the world. These tides have worn away the cliffs to reveal some of the finest fossils from this period.

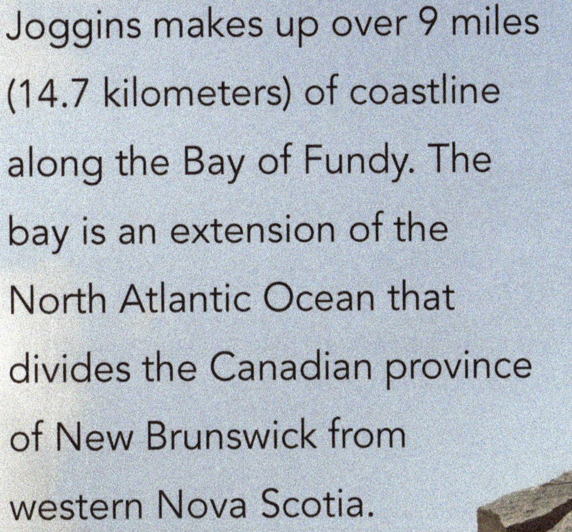

Joggins makes up over 9 miles (14.7 kilometers) of coastline along the Bay of Fundy. The bay is an extension of the North Atlantic Ocean that divides the Canadian province of New Brunswick from western Nova Scotia.

The gray and reddish-brown cliffs at Joggins are more than 98 feet (30 meters) high. The beach is made up of lumps of coal and boulders from the cliffs above. The stone fossils fall out of the coal and are left on the shore when the tide goes out. Where did the coal come from?

During the Carboniferous Period, sometimes called "the Coal Age," huge swamps covered much of Earth's land. Many trees lived in the swamps. The trees were related to plants called ferns that we still have today. Ferns are plants that do not grow flowers or seeds. As these trees died, their remains formed thick layers. Over time, as more layers formed and pressed down on the layers beneath them, the remains turned into coal. Rocks from the Carboniferous Period contain lots of coal.

The first insects with wings appeared during this time.

Larger animals were like today's *amphibians (am FIHB ee uhnz).* They lived part of the time in the water and the other part on land. Many of them looked like the crocodiles that are alive today and were about the same size.

During the Carboniferous Period, where Joggins is today was a *rain forest.* A rain forest is a woodland with tall trees and plenty of rainfall. You can see the fossils of ferns and prehistoric trees at Joggins. Fossil forests stand straight up and down in the cliffs! You can also find fossils of ancient sea life. Tracks from tiny four-legged animals have also been found.

Hylonomus lyelli

Fossils of ancient amphibians and reptiles have been found at Joggins. The *dens* (homes) of amphibians have been preserved with parts of the animals' last meal! In 1852, the oldest known reptile was found buried inside a fossil tree stump at Joggins. The reptile is called *Hylonomus lyelli (HY loh NOH muhs ly EHL ee).* It was found by Nova Scotia-born *geologist* John William Dawson. (A geologist is a scientist who studies how planet Earth formed and how it changes.) The reptile was named after Dawson's teacher, the British geologist Charles Lyell *(LY uhl).* Lyell had also studied the fossils at Joggins. In 2002, *Hylonomus lyelli* was named the provincial fossil of Nova Scotia!

Fossils are fun to find at Joggins. But you cannot keep them unless you get a Heritage Research Permit from the province of Nova Scotia. This is to protect the site for scientific research and to preserve the property for all visitors. If you find something, take a picture of it or let a Joggins Fossil Centre staff member know what you have found. Your discovery could make a valuable contribution to science!

Guides from the Joggins Fossil Centre will show you the property's most famous fossils as well as newly uncovered ones. They can also point out fossils you might miss on your own. The Joggins Fossil Centre also offers several educational programs, activities, and workshops for students from elementary school through college.

In 2008, the United Nations Educational, Scientific and Cultural Organization (UNESCO) made Joggins Fossil Cliffs a World Heritage Site. Some of these places, or sites, are special because of the plants and animals that live there. Others are special because of events in history that happened at them. Governments are required to preserve and protect World Heritage Sites.

JURASSIC COAST

The Jurassic *(ju RAS ihk)* Coast is the United Kingdom's most popular fossil-hunting spot. It lies along the coast of the English Channel in southern England. The Jurassic Coast stretches from Exmouth in East Devon to Studland Bay in Dorset. It covers about 96 miles (154 kilometers). Landslides along the coast have uncovered the fossilized remains of many different plants and animals.

The rocks and fossils found on the Jurassic Coast record the 185 million years of the Mesozoic *(MEHS uh ZOH ihk)* Era. This was a time in Earth's history from about 250 million to 65 million years ago. The Mesozoic Era is often called the time of the dinosaurs. The Jurassic Period was a time during the Mesozoic Era when many well-known dinosaurs lived.

The Jurassic Coast is one of the most important sources of reptile fossils in the world—including dinosaurs! There are fossils of lots of other animals and plants here as well.

At different times during the Mesozoic Era, the Jurassic Coast was a desert, a tropical sea, a forest, and a swamp. In addition to dinosaurs, other reptiles that first appeared during this time included turtles and crocodiles. Early *mammals* also appeared. (Mammals are animals that feed their young on the mother's milk.) The first birds came from small meat-eating dinosaurs during this time. The first flowering plants also probably appeared during this time. At the end of the Mesozoic Era, many animals and plants died out.

The fossils found on the Jurassic Coast help tell the story of some of these animals and plants that have disappeared. The fossils also show us how animals and plants *evolved* (developed over time) in this part of the world during the Mesozoic Era.

Fossils of many different plants have been found on the Jurassic Coast. At the area around Lulworth Cove, in Dorset, there is a fossil forest of tree ferns, conifers *(KOH nuh fuhrz* or *KAHN uh fuhrz)*, and cycads *(SY kadz). Conifers* are trees or shrubs that have their seeds in cones. *Cycads* are large seed plants that look much like large palm trees. Many dinosaurs likely ate these plants!

One of these plant-eating dinosaurs was *Scelidosaurus (sehl uh doh SAWR uhs)*. It is one of the first prehistoric animals ever identified by scientists. Two almost complete skeletons of this creature have been found in Charmouth, in Dorset. It had a long, stout body. Rows of bony plates protected its back, sides, neck, and tail.

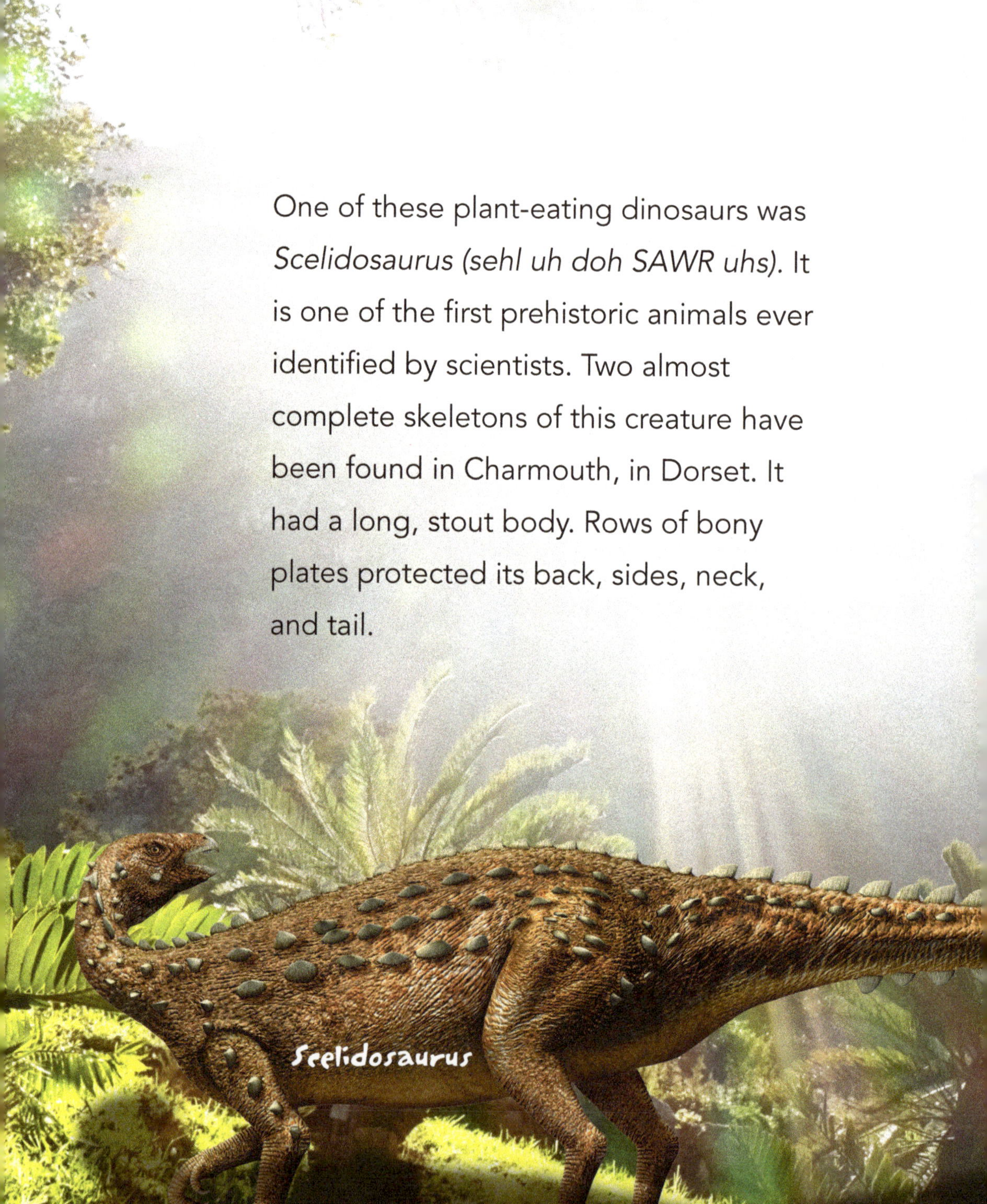

Other reptile fossils found on the Jurassic Coast include those of ichthyosaurs *(IHK thee uh sawrs)*, which looked like fish; large ocean animals called plesiosaurs *(PLEE see uh sawrs)* and pliosaurs *(PLY uh sawrz)*; and flying pterosaurs *(TEHR uh sawrz)*.

Other fossils you may find on the Jurassic Coast include those of fish; hard-shelled animals like lobsters; spiny animals like starfish and sea urchins; and mollusks like clams, octopuses, and squids. The Jurassic Coast is especially known for its beautiful coiled shell fossils of sea mollusks called *ammonites (AM uh nyts)* and *nautiluses (NAW tuh luhs uhz).* Ammonites are extinct. This animal looked like a squid with a spiral shell. Some ammonite shells had ribs, knobs, or bumps. The shell of a nautilus is lined with a rainbow-colored material. Today, nautiluses live among coral reefs in the South Pacific and Indian oceans.

Fossils of insects, amphibians, and a few mammals have also been found here. These mammals include mammoths and hippopotamuses.

fossil mammoth skull

Responsible fossil collecting along the Jurassic Coast is allowed. This is because if the fossils are not collected, they will be destroyed by the sea! It is much better that these fossils are rescued and preserved.

The best and safest place on the Jurassic Coast to try fossil collecting is in Charmouth. There are plenty of fossils there, and you can collect on your own. There are also guided fossil walks from the Charmouth Heritage Coast Centre and the Lyme Regis Museum, in West Dorset. Local museums in the area display some of the most important and spectacular fossils from the Jurassic Coast.

In 2001, UNESCO made Dorset and East Devon Coast a World Heritage Site.

DIGGING FOR FOSSILS

You can find fossils! All you need is a little patience and the right tools.

Here are some tips for successful fossil finding:

- Do not collect fossils unless it is allowed. Check to see if a license or permit is required in the area before you collect.
- Check the weather forecast. Do not go out to collect in rain, storms, or dangerously hot weather.
- The weather and time of year may play a part in helping you find more fossils. You may want to wait until after a rain shower or storm to go fossil hunting. Rain may uncover fossils and make them easier to spot in

some types of rock. Storms may wash fossils onto beaches from deposits in mountain gullies, creek beds, and coastal *bluffs* (high, steep cliffs). In some areas, the middle of winter is the best time to collect fossils. The rough weather may help expose more fossils at this time.

- Bring basic supplies, including:
  - a small geologist's hammer
  - a chisel
  - a steel point
  - hammering gloves
  - a soft brush
  - a magnifying glass
  - newspaper, foam sheets, or other material and elastic bands to wrap fossils for safekeeping or resealable plastic bags and a plastic compartment box with cotton wool for padding
  - a bag or bucket to carry fossils and supplies

- Pick or dig through the rocks. Some people are successful by slowly walking back and forth and looking for fossils that are exposed on the ground.
- Be careful moving about and handling rock. Some types of rock have sharp edges.
- Be careful when digging for fossils in hot weather after mid-afternoon. Rock exposed to day-long sun can be hot to the touch.
  - Wear eye protection, such as safety goggles, especially when you chip away at rock. Rocks can splinter and bits can fly off.
  - Wear long pants, sturdy footwear, sunscreen, and a hat to shade your face.

- Wear a brightly colored jacket or vest and a hard hat in cliff areas.
- Bring plenty of water to drink.
- If you are the grown-up of the group, keep close watch on the kids.
- Do not disturb plants or wildlife. Observe wildlife from a distance.
- Leave the area the way you found it: Take away trash, waste, and food and throw it out (or compost it) in the proper place.

BOOKS AND WEBSITES

BOOKS

Explore Fossils! With 25 Great Projects by Cynthia Light Brown and Grace Brown (Nomad, 2016)
This book takes on fossils, dinosaurs, geology, and ecosystems, as well as the role of scientists in discovering the past.

Fossils by Chris Oxlade (Capstone/Heinemann-Raintree, 2016)
This book gives young fossil fans a taste of the science behind the trilobites and geodes they find. Introduces key concepts, terminologies, and formation processes, along with fact boxes and high-quality, color illustrations. Includes easy-to-understand diagrams captioned photos, and an activity.

Insect Fossils by Barbara M. Linde (Rosen/PowerKids, 2017)
This illustrated book looks at the various ways prehistoric insect forms and trace fossils have been preserved and major modern sites where they can be found. It also describes some interesting discoveries. Includes close-up color photos of fossil specimens.

WEBSITES

Jurassic Coast Official Website
http://jurassiccoast.org/

Includes information for visitors to the Jurassic Coast, as well as a history of the Mesozoic Era. Features a searchable page to teacher training, talks, workshops, and guided walks. A classroom resources page includes a list of subjects searchable by age range. The website also includes a "Fossil Finder" database of around 1,000 fossils from the Jurassic Coast Museums.

Pennsylvania Department of Conservation and Natural Resources
http://www.dcnr.pa.gov/Education/GeologyEducation/IdentifyingandCollecting/Pages/default.aspx

This site from the Pennsylvania Department of Conservation and Natural Resources offers a page on fossil, mineral, and rock identifying and collecting in Pennsylvania. Includes printable fossil illustrations organized by period to help collectors identify fossils.

INDEX

ACKNOWLEDGMENTS

Cover: © Alena Paulus, iStockphoto; © Alice Photo/Shutterstock; © Sementer/Shutterstock; © Sarkao/Shutterstock

2-5 © Shutterstock

6-7 © Shutterstock; © Wild Horizons/UIG/Getty Images

8-13 © Shutterstock

14-15 © Eric Gorski; Montour Area Recreation Commission

16-17 © Walter Myers, Stocktrek Images/Alamy Images

18-19 © Phil Degginger, Carnegie Museum/Alamy Images

20-21 © Aunt Spray/Shutterstock; Didier Descouens (licensed under CC BY-SA 4.0)

22-23 © Nick Hawkins, Nature Picture Library

24-25 © DeAgostini/Getty Images; Public Domain; Ghedoghedo (licensed under CC BY-SA 3.0); © Catmando/Shutterstock

26-27 © Shutterstock; Ghedoghedo (licensed under CC BY-SA 4.0)

28-29 Michael C. Rygel (licensed under CC BY-SA 3.0); © Karen Foley Photography/Shutterstock; © All Canada Photos/Alamy Images

30-33 © Shutterstock

34-35 © Stocktrek Images/SuperStock

36-37 © RapidEye/iStockphoto; © Dorling Kindersley/Getty Images; © Shutterstock

38-39 © Shutterstock; © Alphotographic/iStockphoto; © Kwiktor/Dreamstime

40-45 © Shutterstock

www.ingramcontent.com/pod-product-compliance
Ingram Content Group UK Ltd.
Pitfield, Milton Keynes, MK11 3LW, UK
UKHW061951290726
14090UKWH00021B/1181